My Testimony
Trusting the process
The mindset of a winner

Santiego Rivers

My Testimony:
Trusting the Process

The mindset of a winner

Copyright © 2021 by Santiego Rivers

All rights reserved. No part of this book may be reproduced or transmitted in any form without the written permission of the author.

ISBN 978-1-7370516-4-0

Love-Time -Death

Love is the reason we hate when the emotions that we feel inside feels like a mistake.

Time is the illusion that allows us to think that we have tomorrow when we only have it today.

Death reminds us that life is just a bunch of moments that will eventually come to an end. So death gives time its value.

The question/ the only question becomes what kind of life did we live? Our book of life has many different chapters, but many people get caught up living the same chapters most of their life.

We allow other people to become the authors of our story when they can never give our life the justice it deserves.

The sad parts in our book give our story character and hope that will inspire the reader as they read through the chapters of our book. But, unfortunately, as the writer, we often forget to turn the page and move onto the next chapter in our book because we allow a momentary setback to become more than a moment in our life.

Seconds become minutes, minutes become hours, hours become days, days become weeks, weeks become months, and months become years.

What are you wasting your moments trying to fix that will cause you only to lose valuable time?

Time is the bridge between love and death that we do not have enough of to waste.

Live your life like you are a 24-hour person because tomorrow is only an illusion. When and if tomorrow comes, it will be today.

All the anxiety that you had about tomorrow made you miss out on what you should have been doing today to prepare you for today.

Now you are depressed about what happened in the past that you are allowing to affect you today.

Until you come to understand that every step that you are supposed to take is destined and blessed, you will never find peace in your soul.

On our journey through life, we are never alone. Despite how we may feel and what we may believe, we are loved greater than our understanding of what love truly is.

Love is in it all!!!

All the darkness, despair, anger, and hatred still is centered by love. Without love, how could those other emotions exist?

You must be capable of love to experience all those other emotions.

Darkness and despair come from feeling that you are alone and unloved the way that you desire. Darkness and despair give birth to anger and hatred because of the feeling that love is absent in your life. To feel that love is missing in your life, you must know what love is to miss it from your life.

Therefore, it only makes it logical that love is at the center of all emotions.

So now the problem is, how do we begin to get the feeling of love back in our life? The most challenging questions always have a simple answer.

For us to connect with love, we must first reconnect with ourselves. All journeys start from within. No one can give you something that you already possess.

This book will remind you to trust the process that you will face in life on your journey.

My story will remind you that everyone has obstacles to overcome long as they live. So, what type of life will you live?

My life has been anything but easy, but I wouldn't change it for the world. I have experienced hard lessons and have learned from them all.

I learned that life is what you make it out to be, and no matter what you go through in life, it is the way that you respond to each situation that matters the most.

Life has taught me that responding in anger will never give you the results you need to make you a better person. Instead, responding in anger starts a pattern of dealing with issues that will lead to other problems you may have to face eventually.

Many people are sitting in jail, prison, or resting in their graves because of allowing anger to decide that only wisdom should have made.

For every action, there is a reaction. Are you willing to live with or accept the response from the decision you made while angry or upset?

Will you feel the same way about the decision that you made when you were angry or upset once that feeling or emotion has passed?

Knowledge teaches us that we must figure out what we are willing to accept ultimately.

Wisdom allows us the opportunity to demonstrate the information that we learned from knowledge.

Anger only allows us to momentarily release the pain we feel inside in a negative way.

With anger, one moment can cost you years of your life, if not your life. Many people out there may feel that they do not have a life worth living.

This feeling of hopelessness is because we allowed other people to write the story of our life. We must be willing to take back the pen and begin to write the next chapter of our life.

No person is born thinking negative thoughts about themselves or feeling worthless inside.

Those feelings or things that we allowed other people to fill our mind with has become the thoughts and images that we project to the rest of the world.

Do not let anyone hold you to be the same person you were in the past. Instead, make them respect you by showing them you respect yourself enough to be the person you want to be.

I went from being a male stripper to becoming a certified teacher because I didn't let anyone stop me from doing what I wanted to do in life.

Yes, it took some time to accomplish my dream, and I had to make some significant sacrifices in my life, but I could claim victory because I never gave up on myself.

Learning to believe in yourself is the first thing you must accomplish in your pursuit of rediscovering yourself.

During my self-discovery journey, I can tell you all about how it feels to be on the bottom and the things you see and feel when you are in that situation.

I can also show and tell you how I had to pick myself up and encourage myself to keep climbing until I reached the heights where I can launch to the place I am trying to get.

Knowledge teaches us that the top should never be your final destination. The top should only be your launching pad for you to ascend to new heights. No one jumps from the bottom of the mountain.

Wisdom allows us to apply the gift from the knowledge we learned to find peace in our souls.

My Test, which will become my testimony

I faced losing my job and my wife within the same year/ months. Dealing with just one of those adversities would take your complete focus, energy, and time.

Unfortunately, I did not have that convenience/luxury. Instead, I had to deal with both situations in a matter of months.

If it were not for the knowledge that I learned from going through similar experiences, I would not have been able to apply the wisdom it would take to face my obstacles.

Allow me to tell you about the easiest of the obstacles that I had to face.

(Losing my Job)

I worked for the school district, and budget cuts happen all the time. I understand that no matter how valuable you feel that you are to your company, it is still a business, and you are replaceable/ expendable at the end of the day.

My job/supervisor reminded me of just how valuable I was to the company. I will not go into details of everything I did for my job or all the extra things I did while being employed with Pinellas Secondary school.

The district paid me to do a job, and anything extra that I did while employed at the company is only a reflection of my character as a person.

The way that I feel now about this subject is merely a reflection of when a wise man applies the **knowledge** he has learned over time.

Getting to the point where I am now was not easy, especially with me being so stubborn.

I have learned the hard way that if it were not for the pride that a man carries, he would have no burdens to bear.

I have wasted too much time letting my pride stop me from having peace in my life. I had to learn and accept that my life would only be what I allowed it to be.

I have learned to be determined to allow my life to be beautiful. I want my life to be meaningful and full of purpose. I want my creator to be able to say, *"Job well done,"* when my time here on earth is no longer needed. I would not let any job define or give me my worth as a person.

I serve and answer to a **GREATER BOSS**!!!

The Most High is the only person I am to please.

I loved my job because it allowed me to help one person, which turned into me helping many people over time.

I disliked my job because it allowed me to see and experience how we are failing our scholars in every way.

I admit that I had moments of anger when I knew that I would not be returning to work the following year.

I was mad at my supervisor for not valuing what I brought to the school. I was angry at my co-workers because I felt that they did not work as hard as me, but they would be returning to work next year. The only person that I was not upset with was myself.

(All blame should start and end with us)

When people go through challenging situations, their anger is mainly reflected outwards instead of looking in the mirror at the only culprit who controls everything they do.

What got me through the negative emotions and feelings that I was experiencing is my knowledge and faith in trusting the process. Time will teach us lessons even when we are not ready to learn.

I have learned that what is supposed to happen to us in life will happen. Instead of asking why we need to figure out how we will overcome this obstacle.

We lose valuable time sulking about why we face obstacles in our life instead of coming up with a plan to overcome the obstacle that we are facing.

If not you, then who? Who would you prefer to face the obstacles you are facing in your life? Would you like your most demanding challenges to go to the person you despise the most?

When the person that you tasked with facing your most formidable task prevails and has become stronger and better for it, where will you be?

To be successful in anything, you must be willing to go through or face everything that comes your way.

There is no testimony/ victory without going through a test. If you do not change mentally, you will never change physically.

From my childhood, I remember the story of Job as told within the bible. I recall all the challenges he had to face to prove that he had the **knowledge** and **faith** to apply the **wisdom** that the Highest had blessed him with.

For me, Job's story is a reminder that even if things in your life get tough, you have no reason to be afraid.

Therefore, I smile through this situation that I am currently facing in my life. I have faith that the path that I am supposed to travel is already ordained.

I must apply the **wisdom** to understand that he is opening a new door that I must enter to complete my task when he closes doors on me.

With this understanding, I am currently at peace with this situation. Therefore, I will serve wherever the Highest feels that my service is needed the most.

(Losing my wife)

For better or worse, my wife was one of the best things that happened in my life. She came into my life during a time where I needed someone in my life who would allow me to fulfill my purpose in life.

My purpose in life is to serve/ help people. My wife and I helped each other through some difficult times in our lives.

From the first date with my wife, I knew that I wanted her in my life. I was getting out of a volatile twenty-year, off-and-on relationship with my oldest daughter's mother, and I did not want to get into a relationship with anyone but myself.

If it were not for my wife's stubbornness, we would not have been together. But, in the beginning, we talked and shared pieces of our lives with each other.

I told my wife Somone things that I never revealed to anyone. I told her about my sexual abuse, physical and mental abuse, and suicidal issues.

With my wife, I felt that the Most High knew that I was ready to close one chapter in my life and begin a new chapter.

I had the honor of having Somone Young become my wife. The following are the vows that I wrote that summoned up the past, present, and future challenges that we would face and survive if we stayed under the covenant of the Most High.

My Vows to Somone

Here I stand, shaking and nervous, but still, I am sure. What I want, what I need, I find both things in you. From the moment we met, I knew this would be the last time I fell in love.

I am in love with you. I love who you are and not what you think I want you to be.

I am in love with you. I love the parts of you that make me pause, think and wonder, but never stop loving you as much as I do.

I do.

These words say what love could never mean. **(Commitment)**

I say again.

I do. These words say what love could never mean. **(Commitment)**

As I stand before you and under the covenant of the Most High, I vow to give you my best even when my best may fall short of showing you how much you truly mean to my life. From major to minor, you embody both my wants and needs.

What you mean to me is everything, so I would give you anything to keep you in my life. You became anything and everything that matters in my life the day you did me the honor of being my wife.

You are the one thing that connects the disconnect between my heart and my mind simply because of you.

I admit that, like me, you are not always easy to love, but I love you just the same. Therefore, I humbly say, every rigid piece of you fits perfectly with me and my life. What makes us different are all the things that will ultimately keep us together. Today, tomorrow, and forever, I will find a way to keep you in my life.

You are the here and now that I want in my life forever.

Our Beginning

In the beginning, we faced challenges on both ends. I had to deal with Somone's manipulative and controlling mother, whom I love and respect; Somone had to deal with my ex. She would not leave us alone.

We faced outside challenges in our relationship from the beginning that did not allow us to focus on the only obstacles we needed to care about, which was us.

In our marriage counseling, we learned that we were not going to be in our marriage alone. Our union was going to be under the covenant of the Most High.

> *"Marriage was designed to be a three-way relationship with the Most High in the Middle" – Al Janssen*

This message from the pastor was one of the most important messages that I kept from our marriage counseling.

From our marriage counseling, I learned about creating a honey-to-do-list and how our marriage was always going to be a work in progress that demanded us working together to make it work.

Our marriage was going to be my first union under the covenant of the Most High, and this would be Somone's second.

I was never nervous about marrying Somone. On the contrary, I viewed her as a blessing in my life that I desperately needed.

Somone filled a lot of the void in my life and would challenge me to become the person that I needed to be to make this union work for everyone involved in this union.

For any relationship not to work out, one person is never to blame. It takes two people to argue, and it takes those same people to learn to agree to disagree respectfully.

He who dares not to offend cannot be honest.

When my wife told me that she filed for divorce and she wanted me to sign the papers, I did not fight her about her decision.

I knew that we had issues in our relationship and that she did not come to this conclusion overnight.
(Women are master planners)

I did worry that this final decision came from people outside our marriage who never fully invested in our union.

How can you have a **mother-in-law** whose jealousy of her daughter stops her from being the mother that her daughter is still trying to connect with from her childhood?

How can you have a **brother-in-law** who you would not recognize if you passed him in the street yet he wants to give input on our marriage?

The same goes for her father, who has his issues.

The following day, I signed the divorce papers because of a promise that I made to my wife before and after I read her my vows.

If I fell short of making you feel loved, wanted, needed, and respected, I will step aside.

Yes, I suggested counseling, mentoring, and whatever else we could do to make our relationship work.

The problem that I faced on my end was that If I could not get her to go to counseling for the PTSD issues that she lives with every day, how could I get her to go to counseling so that we can learn to communicate in a way that we both feel is productive?

I loved my wife too much to become the reason that she feels that she was unhappy.

I wanted her to be free and find what she thought she was missing.

Unfortunately, my wife never figured out that happiness comes from the inside, and she has struggled with that void for most of her life.

People will come and go out of your life for many different reasons. If you try to keep someone in your life from walking out the door, you may be preventing the person who is supposed to be in your life from entering.

I spent twenty years of my life trying to make a relationship work that was only meant for a season and not a lifetime.

Time has allowed me the opportunity to learn that you will never get what you deserve if you keep holding onto what you don't deserve.

What you settle for is what you deserve.

I learned the **knowledge** from my mistakes, and I am applying the **wisdom** to my current life.

As you can see, no one life is perfect. So stop trying to be perfect for imperfect people. Even the rarest diamond has many flaws.

Enjoy the good moments in your life, and remember that the not-so-good moments will surely pass.

It's okay to love someone, but you should never love them more than you love yourself.

Putting other people's feelings above yours will only leave you feeling tired and drain. Over time those people will respect the hand more than they appreciate the heart of the person who fulfills their wants and needs.

www.ingramcontent.com/pod-product-compliance
Lightning Source LLC
Chambersburg PA
CBHW071014160426
43193CB00012B/2046